I Truly ♥ This Town

(*Overnight*)

by

Donnie Reckless

The pages of this book were graciously bounded for Donnie's family and friends. Let us remember him as a man who decided to walk into a forest.

On July **14**th **1993,** Donnie Reckless vanished into the Grand Teton National Forest for a hike by his lonesome. Legend Reckless has yet to be seen since his departure. He was known as a sled dog in his community and is greatly missed by those who are blood, and those who are bread.

100% of the material in this book was taken from a private journal belonging to Donnie and not being recovered until early spring of **1996.**

This book is a work of fiction. The characters, incidents, and dialogue are drawn from Bobby's imagination and are not to be construed as real, but rather more than real. Any resemblance to actual events or persons, living or dead, is entirely coincidental and you're thinking too much about it.

First Edition

Cover designed by the author

Library of Congress Cataloging-in-publication has been applied for.

ISBN: 978-1-257-77040-3

Hey, my name is BOBBY but most of the KOONS around here call me DONNIE RECKLESS. I live in BAMMA TOWN, it's south.

Papa bear takes
FLAX SEE oil
NOW, he takes
it in his corn
meal, he eats
on the gator
and goes into
the woods.

yester day →
DADDY(papa bear)
told me I wuz
special, Just
like every
one else. AND
to improve our
NAtion.

TAKE Pills AND
Do drills, we Are
in the army
now. MamMA's
DiSH washing army.
we all really
Love it around
here. Piss.

I Like going
over to Daniel
Stantons house
he has a comp-
uter and we
do chat rooms
on aim and
cyber sex people.

Please help me
and my family
get in touch
with Jesus &
all the good
people he
picks it with.

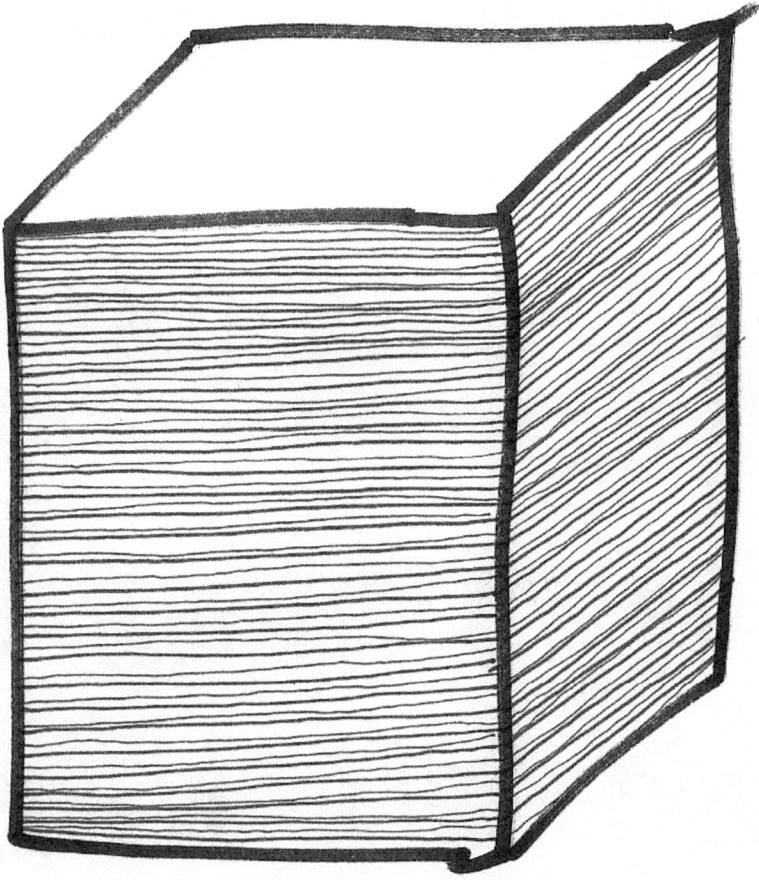

What 10 years of architecture school made
possible

My best
friend got
outta town Last
year, he works
up north mold-
ing salt blocks
for the wild
deer out there.

MANNY MEATBALL
EATS UP ALL
The MEATBALLS
because he
thinks he's in
charge of some
things around
here.

Every morning I have a cup of steaming sauce
rumps skins before I walk the dog or go for a
jogger (dogger)

AUNTY SUSSie
was ALWAY out
in the field
touching her
Moist carry
Back FeuL
StatiON, WET.

WAMP WAMP
DO THE DOOM-
WHAP-DiDDY
JUSt LiKE
chris tucker
DiD it in the
city. MEOW.

Tommis slack
is funny cuz
he always
uses these
snappers to
get his back-
ho purrrring.
But it purrrs.

My Eyes wont
Shut again, I
think my uncle
is gonna give
me his 4x4,
then I'll be
Dirt running.

My Parents
named me big
Don at first
But then I
started stomping
the yard and
they called me
Donnie.

WELL Hey you
again, My DAD
used to MAKE
ME EAT waff-
els and sausage
every morning
till I was
14.

I am Donnie, you should look a little closer

Mom always
cuts out cupons
while daddy
Loads His
shot guns,
I Know HE
Loves Bamma
town too.

I Always en-
joyed watching
Paul Bunion
cook veil over
those hickory
sticks, pickled
possium tail.

Barry wants
MORE Barbie
Wire so he can
make more Under-
ware for His
prisoners, much
More tasteful
then Rail Road
tracks Again

My DADDy sells passenger slots at the train Depot in St. Dellingsville just east of here, we all drink the tap water.

Sometimes I think about going for a hike by myself, I must leave what I Love, I mustn't Love.

My name is Donnie Reck-less but who knows what it will be in a few years, I a really good cook too.

All my life
I've Been
living in a
sandcastle
near I pile
oF Dead Dogs
I feel like.
Stupid dogs.

ALL MY UNCLES
up North have
Their Bug-out
Bags stacked
with much
Love, and canned
Bacon, Lasts for
10 Years!

This bacon lasts for 10 years

Im still in ♥ With Krystile, we only dated for three days but She taught Me HOW to change ▲ Tire.

Donnie has a mother fucking aunt

Donnie has a mother fucking uncle

Theres this rich kid in my town Named darnel and hes got a beefed out honda civic that sounds like a bag of cans getting dragged.

I had to leave
one of my kids
a while back &
I've been try-
ing to find
myself but
theres nothing
that ever changes.

I also really
like watching
the girl at the
bait store bent
over to stock
the cigarettes,
I cream my
union bay's.

I dont take
sugar and I
don't take
cream but I'll
shank a mother
Fucker to blow
of some steam.
chuch.

REAL
iSMM

only .8 cm TALL

If only this wasn't true we'd live for another
1,000 years

Donnie had a freaker fucking father

I wasn't
always normal,
I know that.
I remember
my mom making
me wipe my
astro hole with
corn husks.

Enough said, Hotel Donkey

What got me into this whole mess in the first place

Thank you so much, to everyone who patted my back for this project and to the whole staff at the bait shop, The Hotel Donkey and of course to my teacher at the architecture school, you know who you are.

www.ingramcontent.com/pod-product-compliance
Lightning Source LLC
Chambersburg PA
CBHW070112070426
42448CB00038B/2557